YIELDED
The Posture Of True Love

Howard Bell

Yielded Life
c/o Howard Bell
602-999-5905
yieldedlife.org

Ordering Information:
For details, visit www.yieldedlife.org

Print ISBN: 978-0-578-34231-3

Editors: Kaitlyn Calcote & Mytra Layne

Cover Design & Interior Layout:
Brian Wooten, Brikwoo Creative Group, LLC.
www.brikwoo.com

Printed in the United States of America.

First Edition

Dedication

So often we look at those who are on stages, in the spotlight, in leadership positions or various other demonstrative roles and think of how amazing those people are. Seldom do we take the time to think about the people who helped these people arrive at their destination or achieve their dreams. It could be someone like a janitor who provides an office free of mess for the high-powered executive. It could be the nurse who assists the doctors and patients. It could even be the mother who raised four successful children to become world changers. No matter what the perceived "subordinate" role is, the fact remains that these people deserve to be honored. For this reason, I am dedicating this book to the unsung heroes. These heroes have yielded their lives. They have demonstrated love for others sometimes above their own needs and desires. To these heroes, I want to say, "thank you." This book has been made possible by heroes like you who have helped me achieve so much.

Acknowledgments

I want to expressly state that this book, and much of my life, is only possible because of the faith, love, and support of my father (Jack Bell), mother (Paula Bell), older brother (Mike Bell), and older sister (Dee Dee Bell). God truly gave me living examples of what it means to yield from a posture of love. All of my family has played a role in making sure that I was able to achieve whatever God allowed me to achieve.

Outside of my biological family, who are the foundation of a true example of yielding, there are a few people I must acknowledge. Special thanks and honor goes to all the caregivers in my life. They have been my hands and feet and so much more! Without them, and their sacrifices, I would not be here. Specifically, I want to thank the Baker family. They were there when God first allowed me to share this message, and they encouraged me to find a way to move past my fears to release this message to the world. More recently, and since its inception, Michelle Baker has been one of the strongest forces behind the intercession and encouragement to complete this book. Not only has she spent countless hours in prayer, but she has typed more than half of the book as I dictated it. Thanks, Michelle!

Finally, while I know there have been so many that have helped, I want to thank an individual who literally has taken on my care for the past few years by himself. He means more to me than he'll ever know. He has kept me healthy and safe, with God's help, during my time of writing this book and dealing with some of the most difficult transitions of my life. Steven Camp is and will always be one of the most powerful unsung heroes in my life.

Endorsements

"A message for the nations... this book will change your life."

Eddie James
Worship artist, minister, and founder of Eddie James Ministries, Eddie James Productions, DreamLife, Fresh Wine Records, and Fresh Wine Publishing

Howard Bell gives a perfect glimpse into the purpose and love of God in the life of a true and passionate believer."

Judy Jacobs
Pastor, Author, Speaker, Worship Leader

"Never have I ever heard a more potent teaching, nor seen a more clear and cutting demonstration of what it means to be yielded. I knew after hearing Minister Howard Bell teach on the subject that evening, that were this message to become a book, we would never hear the end of it. Being yielded may not be comfortable, but it is the only way to see God's power fully perfected. Thank you Howard for your continued obedience to God."

DOE Jones
Inspirational Singer, Songwriter

"This Yielded message is a life changer for all who read it. I came to know Howard and this message through a friend and my life has been forever changed. Howard and his walk with God is authentic and the Lord has given him a word for such a time as this. You will not regret taking the time to read this movement. Guess what? You will want to read it again and again."

Amy Wilson
General Manager
WTNB - Christian Television Network Chattanooga

""This book will help you stay yielded to Gods perfect plan for your life and give you spiritual keys to help unlock your true potential and the success you've always longed to experience in every area of your life."

Apostle Dr. Brian W. Alton
Presiding Bishop / Overseer
ICALM - International Covering Alliance & Licensing for Ministries

Table of Contents

Introduction

It was like no other night of my life. I knew what I was about to do would be one of the most humbling and terrifying things I had ever done. At the time, I was forty-four years old. Living life as a quadriplegic had its fair share of challenges, but what was about to happen would prove to be one of the most difficult, yet rewarding, challenges of my life.

I had been slowly making my transition back into the world of public speaking. This is a world I knew all too well. As far back as I can remember, I had been a speaker, spokesperson, or a performer for some kind of church group, special needs organization, non-profit community organization, or activist political cause for advocacy in the area of education. Being in front of people or on camera seemed to always come natural to me. Perhaps it was because I have a passion to see others succeed, but in some ways, it was the easiest way to hide a dark secret – a secret that became so hidden, I almost started to forget it was there. This secret was so dark and toxic, it started to erode into every area of my life. This erosion was not always noticeable in my everyday life, but the evidence of the deeply hidden secret was indisputable.

After over four decades of what seemed, from the outside, to be amazing acts of courage and success to others, I had my moment of reckoning. This moment started this male quadriplegic down a path of personal inventory and self-realization that has been changing my life ever since. I have not kept this journey private. In fact, I have embraced living this journey publically. By doing so, many people are experiencing what it means to awaken their true identity. They are "yielded" (which is the posture of true love) and intentionally activating purpose in their daily living. They are realizing what it feels like to walk in ignited destiny.

That night, three years ago, is the moment when I would finally take the first step to reveal the truth behind the mask of surface-level success. That night, I chose to embrace the concept of yielding to the process through the understanding of truly loving life and who I am. If you are ready to experience the joy of real success, and if you, like I was, are ready to stop living with the feeling of never being good enough, I invite you to read this book and journey with me to discover how yielding through the process will unlock the true success you have been waiting to experience.

And ye shall know the truth, and the truth shall make you free. – *John 8:32 KJV*

CHAPTER ONE

The Reckoning Begins

I laid awake staring at the ceiling. My body literally shook and trembled at the thought of what was about to happen. "What was I thinking?" I said to myself. The commitment was already made. I could not back out now, but everything inside of me wanted to run the other way. Okay, maybe not everything. If I am honest, there was a small part of me that felt a very strong pull toward something. It was something great. Its intensity was strong enough to be felt even among all the fear that I was facing. As I lay there that night struggling to find even two minutes of sleep, I could hear the whispers of fate and a gentle tug of destiny pulling at the strings of the very fiber of my being. It was as though there was a cosmic tug-of-war between my fears and destiny. Some might call it anxiety, but to me, it was tantamount to a World War III epic saga. Thoughts were flying through my head like torpedoes headed toward a submarine in the middle of the battle.

"You're going to look stupid!"
 "Do you realize how weak you will look?"
"What purpose will it serve?"
"They're just going to feel sorry for you."

"This will be so humiliating."

The list of negative self-talk goes on and on. On the other hand, the whispers of purpose and destiny kept piercing through the melee of negative thoughts.

"You were born for this."
"Others need to see a 'Yielded: The Posture of True Love' visual example of what it means to…"
"This is bigger than you."
"What if this one example could be the key to unlocking destiny in someone else?"

It was as though my mind had opposing sides. Each side was hurling missiles at the other. The battle was raging so strong that my physical body began to break out into sweat.

I remember staring at the clock wondering if the morning would ever come. At the same time, I was praying it would not. It wasn't as though I was forced or even pressured to do anything. I guess deep down inside I knew this is what I was, ultimately, purposed to do. In fact, it was that night, with that particular mental battle, when the moment of my true reckoning began.

After many years of public speaking, I lay there that night asking myself, "Why is this time different?" I knew it wasn't the thought that I would be speaking. I knew it wasn't a lack of self confidence in the area of how to construct a message. But what was it? The truth is I knew the answer. The reality was I did not want to hear it at the time. I am not sure why, but it was a question or discussion that I had avoided for many years. That night, with my commitment to speak on the topic of "yielding," I knew it was time to face the secret. It was time to take out the shovel of self-discovery and start digging to get to the core of what I had been burying for years. Over the course of my life, I have had many opportunities to reflect on problems or issues. Often, these times of reflection were mainly during times where I was trying to accomplish a task or review a mistake made during a specific moment or times when I was trying to advise or consult someone else in dealing with their challenge or problem. These times usually served as opportunities to improve or change a specific process in order to increase productivity or produce a positive outcome.

As I look back now, I realize that times of reflection and evaluation have always been a part of my life, but I had quickly learned how to use these times as ways to avoid having to deal with some of the deeper issues in my life. Realizing how I navigated daily tasks throughout my life, I see how reflecting and analyzing had become part of an everyday process. It was rarely used when it came to dealing with the most painful parts of my emotions. I, like so many, had slowly mastered the ability to rely on self-evaluation and reflection to ensure my outward safety and self-preservation. Whether it was evaluating how well I liked a particular food or whether or not I would read a book over for the second time, I knew how to look back and evaluate. On the other hand, self-evaluation and personal inventory was something I avoided like the plague, especially when it dealt with an area of internal imperfection and emotional pain or perceived weakness. As I lay there that night, I had a moment where it was as though the whole world became smaller and my focus became pinpointed on one particular thought. It was the realization I had stayed focused on everything outside of my internal pain. Problem-solving, evaluating, constructing, building, serving others, and staying busy were all good practices I had put into place. I now realize they served as tuxedos worn over an unclean and uncared for inner man. Embracing the process of dealing with what was underneath the fine exterior apparel was more than difficult; it was horrifying! To get to what was underneath, I would need to be willing to become completely exposed. I would have to be willing to take off the tuxedo to get to what lie beneath. Even if I could muster up the strength to begin peeling away at the exterior, it would mean I would eventually have to be willing to look at the naked truth about who I am. It was this truth I was afraid to face. This fear had caused me to bury feelings and opinions about myself so deep that my identity had somehow become lost. My identity had been buried away in the dark while the mask of success and accomplishments took center stage. It was true, in that moment, I realized I had become buried alive.

"How would I ever get out of this self-made coffin where I was finely dressed in the tuxedo of accomplishment and fake self-confidence?" This question was all that I could hear myself thinking that night. I remember continuing to think about what had become the proverbial dirt that weighed so heavily on the coffin I had become so comfortable living inside of. That night, I began to recognize the truth about who I had become. With this truth came an awareness. I had allowed external and internal negative thoughts to become granules of dirt, that when slowly compiled, became the weight and pressure outside of the box (coffin) of self-esteem and self-worth I had built to protect myself. As if that weren't enough, inside of my self-made coffin of protection, I had tried to dress myself in accomplishments and abilities to prove my worth, but who was I proving it to? It was in that moment I realized I had succumbed to the idea that I was unlovable. As contradictory as it may seem, somehow all my accomplishments and achievements could not change or help me deal with the feeling inside that I could not be loved.

It was about daybreak when I reached the point where I could fully understand why this particular presentation seemed so difficult to deliver. This message was about choosing to yield. It was about realizing how many times in our lives we think we are "going with the flow." While that may be true on the outside, there can often remain a continual struggle on the inside. This was true for me. The message I would deliver that evening would be one which would require me to become vulnerable. I would need to admit my life had been full of submission and obedience to events or people, but I was not choosing to believe I could be loved, and I most certainly was not choosing to love myself, which would make it almost impossible to truly yield.

As I prepared to speak later that night, the moment of reckoning from earlier that day brought me to a place of understanding. I now understood that the first step in yielding to any process is to choose to do so through love. That day, I chose to begin to dig my way out of the coffin, to strip off the tuxedo, and begin to love the person within.

I call heaven and earth to record this day against you, that I have set before you life and death, blessing and cursing: therefore choose life, that both thou and thy seed may live: That thou mayest love the LORD thy God, and that thou mayest obey his voice, and that thou mayest cleave unto him: for he is thy life, and the length of thy days:... – Deuteronomy 30:19-20 KJV

CHAPTER TWO

The Exhumation

Early the next morning, as the day got started, I found myself in quite a perplexing situation. My moment of reckoning had happened. The truth was revealed. The posture of my life had been converted from one of love and passion for self and others, to a life of indentured servitude and a mindset of survival. As reality began to set in, I found myself wondering, "Now what?"

Countless questions fired through my mind like a semi-automatic weapon. Questions like:

"How do I get out of this mindset?"
"How did I ever get into this overwhelming position of low self-esteem and lost identity?"
"How will you ever find your way out?"
"How would I begin digging through an endless mound of negative thoughts, negative words spoken over me, and negative belief systems I had become so accustomed to?"

The overwhelming urge to get outside of myself and try to break free from it all seemed to be almost too much to handle. I remember thinking in the moment just how easy it would be to give up and just leave things the way they were. Just as I felt myself entertaining the proposition of leaving things the way they were, I had what some might call an epiphany. Call it an inner voice, a hunch, or the word of the Lord, but in that moment, I heard these words: "The exhumation begins with a word, but the excavation starts within."

Several months prior, in the early days of November, I found myself going to work as usual. The early morning Arizona weather was cool and brisk. Traffic was its normal stop and go as we made our way from my house to my corporate job about twenty-five miles away. It was nothing unusual for me to wake up feeling a little bit congested or lethargic during the fall and winter months. This day was certainly no exception. However, there was a very distinguished difference on this particular day. Accompanying my normal fall allergies was the constant nagging of muscle aches and a restlessness I could not pinpoint. Nevertheless, my assistant, who was riding with me, and I continued toward the office. Although the drive was no longer than usual, it seemed as though the journey was taking forever. In just under an hour, we had reached the office. By this time, my body had begun to give way to chills, and the pain became ever-increasing.

We made our way into the office building and eventually to my office. Over the next hour or so, I did my best to go through the normal daily routine. We arrived at the office around 8:15 a.m. By 9:30 a.m., I could no longer handle the chills or the pain. I drove my wheelchair to my supervisor's desk and let her know that I needed to go to the doctor. I wasn't sure what was wrong, but I knew I had to get help.

Shortly before 10 a.m., my assistant and I pulled into the doctor's office. We had called in advance, so they were expecting me. Surprisingly, we were able to get right in. The nurse did the normal procedures of taking vitals and asking the usual questions about why I was there. As she was taking my temperature, I will never forget the look on her face.

"I am not sure what's wrong with this thermometer," she said. "Do you mind if I take your temperature again?" she asked with the sound of concern in her voice. After taking my temperature a second time, she excused herself from the office. "Please give me one second, the doctor will be right in," she said with urgency.

The examining room door was barely shut for more than 30 seconds before the nurse practitioner appeared on the scene. "Mr. Bell," she said. "You mind if I take your temperature one more time?" she asked with what felt like a fake confidence combined with an eerie concern. "Sure," I said with questioning in my voice. "Is something wrong?" I asked with a shake in my voice while the pain continued to intensify. The nurse practitioner continued by asking me if I knew what day it was and what hospital I preferred to go to. I wasn't able to get the second question answered before the intensity of concern in her voice was no longer masked behind the professionalism of being a physician. She was now recommending that I go immediately to the hospital located in the parking lot of the doctor's office. Apparently, my temperature was just over 104°. Because the hospital was so close, my assistant decided to drive me over.

When we arrived at the hospital, the doctor's office had not been able to call him as quickly as we had arrived. The front office attendant started with their usual protocol of intake. By this time, my pain level had reached the point where all I wanted to do was lay down. I became very forceful with the front office attendant as I requested a bed. The attendant kept insisting that I take a seat and wait to be called. I asked my assistant to call an ambulance while I was in the lobby of the hospital. All I knew is that something was wrong, and I needed to lay down.

The next thing I knew, they were rolling a bed out to the lobby to get me. Suddenly, it was like a three-ring circus. I had nurses, doctors, phlebotomists, and x-ray technicians coming from everywhere. In less than an hour, they had figured out that I had a severe infection in my blood and what looked like a small patch of pneumonia in my lungs. By noon, I was in the Intensive Care Unit/Pulmonary Ward. It was probably 2 p.m. that afternoon when a pulmonologist came in to let me know that they were going to put me in a step-down unit of the ICU because they thought the pneumonia was not what was causing my issues. Fifteen minutes later, they were transferring me to another room of the hospital. While being transferred, my pain, which had been stabilized, began to increase again. As he got me settled in the room, I asked him for something to help with nausea and pain. Less than 10 minutes later, the nurse came in and administered a combination of compazine and morphine. The last thing I remember was thanking my sister for being there as I closed my eyes to go to sleep.

What would take place over the next few days was what I thought was a dream. Little did I know, I was in a coma. Thousands of people were praying for me around the world. All the while, I was literally experiencing what I now know as the beginning of my exhumation.

The walls of the room appeared to be a translucent pale blue and purple rainbow-esque color. The atmosphere of the room was one that I can only describe as total peace, joy, and tranquility. It was as though I was looking through my own eyes, but I could not see my own body. Before me were the faces of loved ones of loved ones whose funerals I had attended or whose funeral services I had preached. Everyone was so happy to see me. I cannot fully remember the conversations, but I do remember how each of them indicated they would see me soon. It was always a group of two or three people at a time.

When the conversation would end, the next group would suddenly appear. It felt like this was happening very quickly, but in actuality, it was happening over a thirty-hour period of time. Somehow, I was experiencing something that would change my life forever. At the end of this experience, I remember seeing my grandma, Bell. She smiled at me and said this is not a dream. "Howard Paul," she said in her grandma voice, you have more to do for God." As she disappeared, I heard a voice saying, "Will you yield?"

My eyes were puffy from the amount of IV fluids they had been putting in me. I could barely pry my eyelids apart to see. As my eyes began to focus, I read the wording on the band that was around my left wrist. I will never forget looking at it. It was purple. The words read, "DO NOT RESUSCITATE." Dazed and confused, I started putting the pieces together. I wanted to speak, but there was a mask over my nose and mouth forcing air into my lungs. With every exhale, I would try to speak. My attempts were futile. The mask suctioned to my face prohibited any attempts I made to speak. My body felt weak. I knew that I was in serious, dire straits.

Over the next few hours, I would make several attempts to communicate. I could hear everyone speaking around me. They knew I was conscious, but I kept slipping back and forth into sleep. Later that evening, I was finally able to begin to speak. By this time, I was able to gather that I had missed at least one day of my life. I was able to understand that whatever had happened to me was so serious that I had nearly died. In fact, as I look back on it now, I might say that I had spent time between life and death.

As the sun pierced through the hospital blinds the next morning, I remember thinking about the events that had been happening. I wondered if it had all been a dream. I couldn't shake the feeling that something so real and supernatural had happened. I was still alive. As the doctors made rounds that morning, they began to explain to me the severity of my situation. The pulmonologist explained how my lungs had filled up with carbon dioxide and my oxygen level had reached critical lows. It was obvious, from the look on his face, I should not have survived. That morning, doctor after doctor came in with updates. Each of the updates were pretty much the same. All the doctors had the look of astonishment and bewilderment on their faces. Their message and tone was clear. Without acknowledging a medical miracle, they all pretty much acknowledged the same thing. In fact, one of them summed it up well when he said, "You are obviously not done here yet."

That day, after all the doctors had finished their morning rounds, I found myself revisiting the events of the past few days. "Could it have been a dream?" I said with a low voice. Somehow, I knew it was too real to be a dream. I knew it was more than a

dream. Deep down inside, I knew what I had experienced was an encounter with the supernatural.
Some might say it was my fundamentalist Christian
upbringing, some might say it was simply a dream,
others might even say I was having a drug-induced
hallucination, but the events of that day and the
question I was asked would not leave my mind.
The question, "Will you yield?" rang so loud in my
thoughts. It did more than breach the annals of my
mind; it reverberated through every essence of my
being.

For the next few days, I pondered the question. To
be honest, there were times during that week of
recovery where I got angry about the question. I
knew the voice behind the question was God. There
are some who argue His existence and the idea He
actually speaks, but that day, there was no doubt. I
knew the Creator, a spiritual being called God, or
to some, a higher power, had placed a call. The call
came in the form of a question. It was a question,
quite honestly, that I found to be offensive at first.

"Will I yield? Is this some sort of a joke?" I modelled
those words under my breath over the next few days.
I mean, how much more yielded could an individual
like me be? My entire body has full sensation from
the neck down, but no strength to do anything in
most areas. I can't even urinate without help. I have
to be cleaned up when I use the restroom. I have to
be fed. I have to be turned over at night. Someone
has to help me use the phone. The list goes on and

on, yet I am being posed with the question, "Will you yield?" I could not stop myself from thinking this was some sort of sick joke.

For several months, my anger clouded the revelation of what this question would ultimately reveal. I didn't realize it then, but I was filtering the question through years of offense that had built up. It was distorting the question posed in love into an accusation of failure. My mind had twisted the very question that would begin the exhumation of my spirit from the coffin of low self-worth and lost identity. For the next several months, the question would continue to pull me forward. As the anger slipped away like dirt falling off and as my body was being lifted from the depths of the grave that had been sealed with offense, I suddenly found myself desiring to know more about what it meant. What was the voice really asking me?

Several months culminated to this one point. This was the day when my exhumation would be made official. I was now being asked, by that same voice, to present the question to the world. For the first time, I would be sharing some of the discoveries made during my time of exhumation. Little did I know, that night would be the opportunity for me to experience freedom, and it would also be the beginning of the second part to answering the call. It wasn't enough for my coffin to be brought up and out of years of offense; now, I had to choose to love–to love myself enough to disrobe from the dirty tuxedo of false confidence, and to love others enough to share the demonstration of yielding through my life. Now it was time for me to choose to get out what was inside. Now, it was time to be exposed and vulnerable.

---

*But he knoweth the way that
I take: when he hath tried me,
I shall come forth as gold.*

– Job 23:10 KJV

CHAPTER THREE
Digging for Gold

Yep! There was no way out now. I had only two hours left before I would speak. My notes were pretty basic. I was often known to keep notes in my head, but this time, I actually had someone help me write down an outline, so I could see it. I'm not sure why. I honestly knew the reality was this night would be a complete heartfelt delivery. It is not that all of my deliveries from the past were not; it was just this one was coming from a place of vulnerability and transparency that I had never displayed before. As the time grew closer, I practiced breathing deeply and praying. As I was praying and meditating, I began to reflect on the weeks leading up to this moment. There was one particular moment where I knew that eventually I would be delivering this message. A smile breached my face as I recalled the incident.

I was preparing to teach a local Bible college one night. As my caregiver was dressing me, we began to discuss my class content. At the time, I was talking about identity. Specifically, I had been teaching a three-week course on Kingdom Identity. This was the final week of my course, and I was going to be talking about choosing to believe who we are. I'm not exactly sure how the conversation started that night, but I do remember reflecting on it. The most memorable moment of that night was when my caregiver had picked me up to place me in my wheelchair. She began to talk to me about the idea of how before she and her family ever came to take care of me, they thought they understood caregiving. She went on to describe how taking care of me had opened their eyes to what it meant to truly care for someone in the way that they needed to be cared for and not in the way that she thought was best. We began to discuss how, from the perspective of a caregiver, she had really begun to understand the love of Christ and the way He cares for us. She then started to ask me if I had ever considered what it would be like to use my body as a demonstration of how much trust and love we get to have for those who are caring for us both temporally and spiritually.

"I will never do that!" I said with a raised voice. I'll never forget the look on her face as she was carrying me. "Why not?" she asked. "It is just too humiliating. I'm skinny. I have to have help to go to the bathroom. I have a curved back, and people are already looking at me as different. I do not want to get out of my chair and look completely limp in front of people," I said with tears in my eyes. The look on her face was one of complete shock and compassion. "I do not believe people would look at you that way at all," she said with tenderness. "Please just stop talking about it," I said with agitation. It was obvi-

ously a moment of preparation in my life for what
was to come.

All at once, I found myself back in the room where
I was praying and meditating. My mind, for a brief
moment, drifted back to remind me of how God had
set all of this in motion. "Well, isn't this just one of
life's ironies?" I said with a chuckle. That night, just
under six months later, as I meditated and prepared
to deliver the message, the same caregiver sat next to
me. "What do you mean?" she said. I asked her if she
remembered the night when we had talked about
me getting out of my chair to demonstrate what it
meant to be yielded to God. A big smile stretched
over her face as she said, "Yes." "Well, you must've
been somewhat prophetic, because tonight will be
that night!" I said with excitement. She immediately
sprang into action with questions and preparations.
We began collecting a blowup mattress and other
items I would need to effectively pull this off.

As everyone was hustling around trying to get me
ready for the evening, which was quickly approaching, time seemed to stand still. I knew I was going
to be physically vulnerable and become a visual aid
for God to use for His glory, but I was also going to
become vulnerable emotionally and spiritually. As
I mentioned earlier in this book, the night leading
up to this presentation was truly an epic battle. Not
only was I about to bear it all physically, but God
had dealt with me about exposing my own self-esteem issues through the act of forgiveness and

repentance. That night, I would also ask a friend of more than twenty years for forgiveness. I would do this in front of more than 300 people in attendance. The excavation from within could only be accomplished by me choosing to let go of past hurts and wounds and to ask for forgiveness for carrying jealousy for more than twenty years. The man who invited me to speak that evening was not only a well-known gospel artist, but he had been my best friend 20 years ago. This event was actually a sort of reunion. Just over 20 years prior, he and I had traveled throughout Arizona, New Mexico, Oklahoma, and parts of Texas with his gospel choir. We had seen two pretty miraculous events and shared great visions of what God would do in the future. Then, it felt like nothing could stop us from doing what we were doing together. I didn't know it then, but my character was not advancing at the rate that my best friend's destiny was propelling him forward. He began to travel the world, fulfilling the visions and dreams that had been shown to both of us in our early 20s. As I stated, I did not know then that I had already started putting on a tuxedo to cover up my own insecurities. Nevertheless, when my best friend was stepping into his destiny, my own character flaws and twisted thinking allowed a doorway for bitterness to come in. It wasn't long before bitterness gave way to jealousy. It was a jealousy and wound that had laid so deeply buried I almost forgot it was there. The only time I would feel it would be when I would catch a glimpse of him on television or hear a story of how success and ministry was going for him.

The night leading up to my message was not only the night when I realized that the question to yield would be presented through my physical body, but it was also the night when I realized how much my spirit needed to yield to love. When I realized I had been carrying years of jealousy and unforgiveness, everything in me wanted to let it go. For the first time, I realized how God's love had actually been the reason why I did not go on the journey at that time with my best friend. God knew the path He wanted me to be on to experience the destiny He had for me. That night was not only a night where I would deliver a message which would begin to unlock destiny in my life and the lives of others, but it would be a night of restoration and reunification.

As we made our way into the church that night, my heart was filled with expectancy and a deep reverence I had never felt before. The expectancy was no doubt from the anticipation of what it would be like to deliver a message that required me to get out of my chair. The reverence came from the sense that something larger than me was about to occur. I knew the weightiness of the situation was not from fear, but rather, from a strong desire to bring God glory and honor through my actions.

As the service started, the intensity began to build. I could feel my inner man beginning to dig away at the years of offense and unforgiveness. The excavation was beginning. The gold that would be discovered was beyond anything I could ever imagine. The time was quickly approaching as the song portion of the service began to wind down. My friend of over twenty years began his introduction of me. The moments that would follow would change my life forever.

I beseech you therefore, brethren, by the mercies of God, that ye present your bodies a living sacrifice, holy, acceptable unto God, which is your reasonable service. – Romans 12:1 KJV

CHAPTER FOUR
Defining the Yield

I was shaking and trembling. It was as though what was inside me was boiling and ready to pour out. Tears started to well up in my eyes as I began to speak from the place in my heart that had been buried for so long. "I need to start this by doing something I've never done before," I said with my voice trembling. "You see, I've been carrying something for over 20 years, and I won't be able to deliver tonight's message without addressing it first." I continued.

As I spoke, the crowd seemed to get quieter with every word. I went on to explain how I had been carrying jealousy and unforgiveness toward the man that had invited me to speak that night. The man, who had been my best friend 23 years prior, was the very man to whom I was referring. I explained to the audience how his talent and character had enabled him to carry out some of the visions and dreams we had shared together. "It was difficult to see the rise of his success and not be there with him to experience it," I said with tears streaming down my face. I continued to explain how that in preparing for tonight, I realized how much my character had not been ready all those years ago. In all honesty, I confessed that my character was sorely lacking back then. I asked him to forgive me for holding jealousy and bitterness.

I'll never forget the look on his face. It was a look of complete compassion and surprise. Though he didn't speak, his actions and expressions conveyed the message clearly. I had already been forgiven. The hand over his heart and smile on his face made that clear and obvious. Love had filled the room.

The tone had been set. It wasn't enough for me to ask for forgiveness for my own behavior. That night, I stood in proxy for all the individuals and family members in attendance who had held bitterness, jealousy, and unforgiveness toward this man. The night was meant to be a reunion, but it was also a night of reconciliation. I wasn't sure why at the time, but I could tell by the look on several faces, this moment was nothing short of supernatural. All over the room, heads nodded in agreement and eyes were full of tears. That night several people let go of some of the baggage they were holding. Those few minutes alone could have sealed the whole evening, but the message was not complete yet. The atmosphere of the room was tender and charged with an overwhelming sense of love, a love that can only come as a result of choosing to yield.

Mustering all the strength I had, I cleared my throat to continue. "Ladies and gentlemen, I would like to continue to share with you what is on my heart this evening," I said with as much competence as I could muster up in the moment. The room was filled with sounds of sniffles and the shuffling of people regaining their composure.

Once again, everyone's attention was beginning to focus on the words I spoke. That night I continued to explain to the audience how my act of repentance was simply a prelude to the introduction of the message I came to share. "Tonight, I would like to speak to you about yielding," was the opening line to the continuation of my message. To fully understand yielding, the atmosphere of love must be present. So, it was only fitting to start with an act of love such as repentance and reconciliation.

For many months leading up to that night, I had pondered and studied the word "yield." As mentioned previously in this book, that word was the heart of the question I had been asked during my near-death experience. Initially, I thought the word meant to simply comply with or follow the directions of someone or something of greater strength or authority. The more I studied and the deeper I dug, I discovered my definition of the word was sorely lacking. What my definition was missing was the context of the mind or will of the individual. The word "yield" carries with it the idea of choosing to align one's will or desire. To make the choice to submit, obey, or comply can come from a place of fear or love. What I had come to discover was that yielding without love is not possible. This is because if love is not present and not the main motivator behind the choice, then the decision to obey, comply, or submit is made from a place of fear. This fear leads to a feeling of slavery, imprisonment, and ultimately, death.

As I continued my message that evening, I felt it necessary to not only share the events of my time in a coma, but to expound on what I discovered about the meaning of what it means to yield. That night, I shared a story of what it looks like to comply while not yielding. Sometimes, it is easier for us to understand what something is not before we can understand what it is. I continued by telling the story of Johnny who was riding in the back of his mom's car at the age of five.

Johnny's mom looked in the rearview mirror and saw him standing up while she was driving. She says to Johnny, "Please sit down, son." Johnny keeps on moving around and standing up. Johnny's mom says more certainly, "Son, I need you to sit down right now!" With all of his excitement and childlike energy, Johnny continues to play around in the backseat. All at once, Johnny's mom raises her voice to a tone that would get his attention. "Johnny, if I have to pull this car over..." Johnny's eyes locks on hers in the rearview mirror. He knows she is not joking. He crosses his arms, takes a deep breath, and slams himself down onto the seat. A few minutes later, Johnny's mom looks into the rearview mirror. She sees him with his eyebrows furrowed and arms crossed. She says, "Thank you for sitting down." Johnny looks at her in the rearview mirror and says, "I may be sitting down on the outside, but I want you to know that I am still standing up on the inside."

The audience let out a chuckle as I finished with my anecdotal analogy. I continued to explain how Johnny reflects how many of us think we are yielding, but we are actually just obedient and compliant. The story of Johnny, though funny and rudimentary, is a good depiction of how I would explain the way I approached many things in my life. I would often do things because I had to or because it was the "right thing to do." Choosing to make these decisions was not always done from the place of love. Very often, it was done from a place of fear of consequence or the feeling of not having a choice. In these situations, these decisions to comply would often lead to a feeling of burnout, enslavement, or even numbness comparable to death.

I asked the audience how many of them felt the same way. "How many of you have found yourself taking a job because you had to, learning in school because you had to, or even serving God because you have to?" These types of questions are what we often ask ourselves when we feel like there will be some negative consequence or result if we choose not to. If we choose not to work, we go hungry or just remain poor. If we don't go to school, then we will remain ignorant, and no one will hire us. If we don't go to church and serve God, then we could spend an eternity in hell and experience eternal damnation. All of these "if/then" statements produce a mindset of compliance and obedience where the choices are made from a place of fear of loss or negative consequences. This type of fear often leads to a life devoid of happiness. This is where I found myself far too often. How does it change? What does it really mean to yield? The answer to this question is not simple enough to wrap up into one definition. Another great example of yielding can be seen in the rules of driving a vehicle. We see the signs on the side of the road asking us to yield. Many of us will slow down, and some of us will speed up to make it through the yellow light. These traffic lights and yield signs are meant to be visual indicators of a possible change in the flow of traffic. When we see them, we are meant to take an assessment of our surroundings, such as oncoming traffic, and adjust accordingly. Failing to make these adjustments can often result in traffic accidents, or even worse, someone could die. The same is true of our everyday lives. When we fail to assess our surroundings and simply choose to do something because we must, the result is much the same.

Yielding requires us to align our will with what is going on and make the choice to adjust accordingly. What does it look like to align with what is going on? What does it mean to truly yield oneself to the process? What are the outcomes? Where do we start? All these questions were easily seen on the faces of everyone in the audience that evening. Even more importantly to the "what," "where," and the "why" questions is the "how" question. As I mentioned earlier, yielding from a place of fear is not, under our definition, yielding. Yielding happens when our choice is made from a posture of love. That evening, it was love for my brother and friend that caused me to ask for forgiveness in front of everyone. It was love for the masses that would drive me to allow my own physical condition to become an example of what choosing to yield from a posture of love looks like. It was now very clear to me why I had been given the choice to deliver this message and why I would be using my own body as an example. I now knew that the call to yield was not just a call that was given to me on one night as I slipped into a coma. It was a call that had been sent out since the fall of man in the Garden of Eden. It was a call of love. It was a call to be loved and to have the choice to make the decision without fear or condemnation. It would not be enough for me to simply share the call that took place during that faith-filled night in the hospital a few months prior. I would need to go back and understand where the call to yield all started.

And he went a little further, and fell on his face, and prayed, saying, O my Father, if it be possible, let this cup pass from me: nevertheless not as I will, but as thou wilt. – Matthew 26:39 KJV

CHAPTER FIVE
From Garden to Garden

Having been raised in a fundamentalist Christian family, much of my worldview had been sculpted through a filter of faith and belief in a very real God. I still hold true to that faith and practice many of the beliefs framed within the context of that worldview. It is no wonder that in the months leading up to that night, I would turn to my faith to find the answers.

When I first heard the voice posing the question of whether I would yield, my initial reaction was one of anger and confusion. I pretty much felt as though it was a personal insult to even ask me such a question. Quite frankly, I cannot use the restroom without having assistance. I'm not able to make a phone call without help. Almost everything I do requires the help or assistance of someone else. To me, I have no choice but to yield all the time. I thought "yielding" was before I began this journey of learning what it truly means.

My research and quest for understanding had illuminated a different meaning of the word as my anger switched to a deep curiosity. I started searching for understanding. Naturally, I looked first to my faith. I began to wonder if I was the only one God had posed this question to. I soon realized, I was not. I discovered mankind was originally created from love, by love, to live in love with its Creator. That's right; I found myself back in the Garden of Eden with Adam and Eve. This is where mankind deviated from a yielded lifestyle and began to live a life of death enslaved by fear.

I continued my message by explaining how I began researching the idea of yielding and how the research took me back to the beginning. "So, there I was in the book of Genesis right around the third chapter," I said to the audience that night. I continued by explaining how I remembered the stories of Adam and Eve from my childhood.

I recalled the usual story of how Eve ate of the apple, and Adam followed suit. I always knew the fruit was not really an apple, but it wasn't until now when I would completely come to understand the depth of the revelation that happened in Genesis Chapter 3. This passage is a story where Eve and the serpent began to have a discussion regarding the tree of the knowledge of good and evil. The Bible talks about how subtle the serpent was and how Eve was beguiled by him. Many preachers, including myself, will often preach from this passage to discuss the fall of man. However, there is something deeper revealed when one takes a closer look at the story. When God originally made man, He placed him in the garden and gave him dominion over the earth and all living things. Everything God created was good. Interestingly, the only thing that was not good was that man should be alone. This means that God and mankind dwelled together in goodness. Man did not need to work in the sense of putting forth effort or any form of pain. He simply needed to walk in the dominion for which he was created.

Mankind had been created by love because God is love. He was created in the image and likeness of love. This means love created mankind in the likeness of love to produce love. This is evident when the Bible refers to God walking with man in the cool of the day. Mankind started out with a relationship made in love, by love, to produce after its own kind. In fact, the only command given to Adam regarding his purpose was for him to be fruitful and multiply. Simply put, love was to be reproduced exponentially.

What was it that happened? How did mankind (Adam and Eve) go from a dominion-based relationship with the love that created them to a death sentence? The answer lies in a decision made. In one moment, one decision changed everything. For years, I used to believe it was the act of disobedience to God's commandment that caused sin and death to reign on earth. Now, a new revelation is suddenly illuminated. Yes, there was definitely disobedience involved, but with true love there is no record of wrong, so disobedience alone could be forgiven.

What was it about eating of the tree of knowledge of good and evil? What could cause a complete trajectory shift and unleash the pandemic of sin that would take generations of sacrifices to cover? The answer was right in front of my face the whole time. I just could never see it until now. Now, when I had a hunger to find out what yielding really meant, there it was. Eve and Adam chose to yield to the voice of something other than love. They chose to yield to the voice of temptation and ate of the fruit of knowledge of good and evil. The knowledge gained from eating of the tree, produced the fruit of self-awareness, self-preservation, and shame that resulted in fear. Mankind was made to yield to its Creator and to walk in dominion over the earth and every living thing. Before eating of the tree they chose what was good because what was good was all they knew. Suddenly, Adam and Eve began to find themselves hiding, covering up and feeling fear because they now had knowledge of good and evil. They now processed things through a lens of "self." Their newfound revelation caused them to hide from their Creator, who was the embodiment of love.

I could hardly contain myself. The more I read Genesis Chapter 3, the more I realized how one act of choosing not to yield to love opened the door for fear to ravish mankind who was never meant to be able to deal with fear. After Adam and Eve had eaten of the tree of the knowledge of good and evil, the Bible says that they were naked and ashamed. It also says that they hid themselves because they were afraid. This is the first time the concept of fear is even introduced. It suddenly made sense.

The New Testament tells us that God has not given us a spirit of fear. It also tells us that there is no fear in love and perfect love casts out all fear. How did this fear suddenly appear? It was because the fruit gave mankind the ability to judge or determine right and wrong. With that ability, everything that was good can become reevaluated. Nakedness, that which was once normal, now brings shame. God, who man used to walk with, is now feared. With the knowledge of good and evil, mankind now understands, for the first time, that he is uncovered. This act of disobedience, alone, could not separate him from love, but the ability to understand good and evil meant man now had a divided mind. Love and fear could now coexist in the same mind or body. Eating the fruit started an epic battle in the mind and spirit of man. He was now faced with having to choose whether to yield to love or yield to fear.

The more I studied, the more I realized the depth of God's love and desire for us to be yielded to Him. Soon after Adam and Eve had eaten of the tree, God came calling out to Adam. I found it interesting that God would ask Adam where he was. How does an omnipotent, omniscient, and omnipresent Being not know where His creation is? Perhaps, it wasn't a question for knowledge sake. It was, quite possibly, a question for Adam and Eve to assess where they were in relationship to the posture of love. Perhaps a loving God felt the love a father feels when he knows the ramification of an immature act performed by one of his children. This could be the very reason why the Bible says God put them out of the garden so they would not eat of the tree of life. It was an act of mercy to remove them from the garden. God did not want man to live forever with the battle that rages between fear and love.

The more I thought about the fall of man in the Garden of Eden and the desire God had to be with mankind, the more the depth of God's love became revealed. Though I had been in church my entire life, I was now over forty years old. For the first time, I was just discovering new depths of how God has always desired for us to choose love.

The more I searched the Bible, I found the threads of God's plan leading the way to yet another garden. This time, my pursuit of what it meant to yield took me to the Garden of Gethsemane, a passage where Jesus and the disciples went away into the garden. Jesus asked his disciples to stay close by while He went to pray. The Bible says He prayed and cried tears of blood regarding what was about to take place. It is this conversation Christ had with his Father that became so striking. Jesus said, "I would that this cup pass from me, nevertheless not My will but Your will be done." At this moment in the garden, Christ was faced with choosing to yield to the fear of death or to the passion of love, a love so great it would lay down its life as an example and as a covering to forever clothe the nakedness exposed by yielding to fear in the Garden of Eden.

The conversation Christ had with God the Father was to set the example of how we can choose to yield to the will of the flesh (fear) or choose to yield to the will of God (love). Christ's choice took Him to a tree where the posture of love was demonstrated by presenting Himself as a sacrifice. It is interesting to note how mankind was introduced to the posture of fear by a conversation which took place at one tree in the Garden of Eden, and it was introduced to the restoration of eternal love at another tree placed on Calvary. The conversation prior to Christ making the ultimate sacrifice was the supreme example of what yielding from a posture of love looks like. The Bible says He presented Himself and gave His life for our sins.

At this point, I could hardly continue my research. I had discovered the love of God in such a different way. I realized the biggest revelation of Calvary, at least for me, was the decision made in the Garden of Gethsemane. Christ could have chosen to back out. The Bible tells us He endured the pain of the cross for the passion that was set before Him. That passion was a love for me and whoever else believes. My heart was so overwhelmed with this new understanding I could hardly continue. I just wanted to bask in His love, but something was telling me to go deeper. I understood Christ's opportunity to give in to fear and His decision to yield to the plan of God in His love. I could clearly understand His drive in a way I had never seen. For the first time, I understood how the humanity of Christ was setting the example for us. His humanity felt the pain and fear of the weight enduring the cross would bring, yet He chose to yield by presenting Himself to the cross. By doing this, we gained something back in the Garden of Gethsemane that mankind had forfieted in the Garden of Eden. Mankind regained full access to eternally walk with God in the cool of the day. By Christ choosing to yield to the will of the Father, He was showing mankind to choose love over fear and life over death.

This newfound revelation caused me to look deeper into the power of yielding. Yes, Christ came as the example, but how does it apply to life today? I was pleasantly surprised to find that the apostle Paul covers it well in Romans 12. Paul is pleading with fellow Christians and asking them to "present" their body as a living sacrifice. No doubt Paul was making this plea knowing that Christ, who is our supreme example, had already set the model in place. Christ gave His body as a sacrifice, and here in Romans 12, Paul is asking us to do the same. Why? It is to prove the will of God and the will of love, which has no fear. Fear enslaved mankind to death until Christ came and rendered it powerless by not yielding to fear. This fear is what Paul refers to as the "bondage of fear." The first place we see mankind's fear is in the Garden of Eden when they ate of the tree of the knowledge of good and evil. Some years later, the

apostle Paul talks about how we have been freed
from this bondage. He tells us that we received a
spirit of adoption where we can cry, "Abba Father!"
I suddenly realized, as I continued studying, that the
apostle Paul was not only talking about freedom
from fear, but he was also giving us a key to how to
establish the dominion and authority we had let go
of in the Garden of Eden. The key was right there in
Romans 12. The apostle Paul pleads for us to present
our bodies as a living sacrifice. As I looked closer,
I found myself focusing on the word "present." To
my surprise, the word translates to the word, "yield."
Could it be that the apostle Paul was, in all actuality,
telling us the power of proving the will of God is
through yielding? The act Christ demonstrated in
Gethsemane's garden is the same act that is the key
to demonstrating the will of God on earth. It is the
act of yielding by making the choice to willingly, and
from love, choose to present ourselves fully to God.
The depth of love it takes to say, "Here I am; do with
me what you will," starts with one choice. It is simple, but it is one of the most difficult things for mankind to do. Making the choice to completely allow
God to care for us and believe that He has the very
best in store for us is the one thing that the enemy
(the devil) has been trying to stop from the beginning. Why? It is because he knows the true power
and authority that comes from a complete unifica-
tion and alignment with God when we present our
bodies, soul, and spirit completely to His care.

Jesus' act of yielding (presenting His body, soul,

and spirit) in the Garden of Gathsemane resulted in the redemptive reunification of God's original plan to walk alongside His children and care for them. A choice of yielding that Adam and Eve could not make in the Garden of Eden after they had eaten of the tree is the choice that created a gulf between heaven and earth, life and death, and God and man. This gulf was suddenly removed by Christ's act of yielding. It was not only the act of Calvary that won our salvation. It was also, and probably most often missed or overlooked, the choice Christ made in Gethsemane's garden to yield to His purpose and passion over His earthly desires. Had He not willingly chosen to endure or face the cross, but do so under strict obedience, I believe the result would have been much different. It would not have been an act of yielding made from love; it would have instead been an act of responsibility made from fear. It was this act of love that served to be powerful enough to drive out all fear for future generations to make the choice to yield out of love. How does that look?

Trust in the LORD with all thine heart; and lean not unto thine own understanding.

– Proverbs 3:5 KJV

CHAPTER SIX

Presenting in the Present

I could feel the lights beating down on me as I continued to speak that evening. I wanted to share everything I had discovered, but the evening did not afford enough time. The revelation of how Christ gave the example to yield was great in the concept of understanding salvation, but there was so much more. The act of the yielding displayed by Christ afforded access on an eternal level, but there was also a reclaiming of temporal dominion that happened through yielding. There is something more to the concept of presenting ourselves continually to our Creator. I wanted to share everything I had discovered and was currently discovering. That evening I explained how the more I studied, the more I wanted to understand what it would look like to yield. My pursuit of the answer to this question kept me searching deeper and deeper.

That night, I explained how I began to ask question after question inside myself. I could only imagine how others would have the same questions. Questions like: What does yielding look like? Is the act of confession during salvation the only act required in the yielding process? There were many other questions racing through my mind, and I can only imagine the questions that might raise to the minds of those who were hearing what I was sharing. This was probably the most piognant question: What does it look like to yield? I knew Christ's example and I understood how the disciples laid down their lives for the sake of the Gospel, but what would that look like today? The answer to this last question is the one that brought the idea of yielding right down to my very own life. It was like an epiphany happened while I was studying. The thought occurred to me: "My very own life is an example of yielding in the physical." As a quadriplegic, I daily find myself in situations with opportunities to yield. I rely on care-givers, who are much stronger and physically able than I am, to perform even the basic daily functions of life. I get the opportunity to choose to yield to their care or yield to the fear of being without help or care. In much the same way, we get to choose to present our lives to a Creator that is love or choose to yield to the fear that comes through self-reliance and sin.

As someone who depends on others for life's functions, I know how difficult it is to totally present myself to someone for every need. Someone must assist me with eating, using the restroom, getting dressed, bathing, and basically every other function of life. Entrusting that care to someone when love is not present is a very fearful thing. It makes totally presenting myself to them almost impossible. However, when love is present on both sides, yielding is easy.

When love is not present, the quality of care and the experience of life can be miserable. As a quadri-plegic, in the physical, it is easy to understand how self-reliance or total independence is unrealistic. I daily choose to yield to those who care for me. This yielding occurs because I understand the value of receiving loving care from those who can do things when I am not able.

With this realization, I was able to begin to under-stand Christ's example and Paul's request through parallels in my own life. Was I presenting or yield-ing my life to God from the posture of love? Was I honestly understanding the value He brings to my daily life? Did I truly understand His strength to care for me in areas of my weakness? The answers to these questions could only be realized when I began to explore the different areas of life where I had the opportunity to yield. This began to happen when I started viewing God as the ultimate caregiver. The idea that the Creator of the universe loves me and all of His children so much that He created us to be interdependent on His care opened my eyes to see what choosing to yield to His care means. He wants us to need and trust Him just as we want our chil-dren to need and trust us. This revelation opened up a whole new world to me.

I began to draw parallels to my physical life and connect them to the spiritual act of yielding. In fact, one of the first acts of yielding took place that night as I continued to speak. I chose to use my quadriplegic body to demonstrate the parallels. I was choosing to deny the desires to giving into the fear of what others may think about my body, how frail and broken it might look, or how embarrassing it might be. Instead, that night, I was choosing to present my body from a place of love for the body of Christ to demonstrate how much our Creator desires to care for us.

"Tonight, I want to present to you, in the present, what it might look like to yield," I said with a tremor in my voice. "How many of y'all have ever wondered what it may look like to present your body as a living sacrifice?" I asked as the sweat began to pour down my head. I had just spent about fifteen to twenty minutes sharing about the garden experiences from the Bible, and now, it was time to bring those parallels into the present. All of a sudden, the voices of fear and self-awareness began to fade away. A surge of excitement and boldness began to consume my body as I invited my caregivers to the stage. "I would like to share with you through a demonstration utilizing my own body to represent the believer and my caregivers to represent God," I continued. As preparations were being made around me, I continued by explaining how before any portion of my care could be conducted safely when I'm in my chair, it is best to turn the power to my chair off so no one gets hurt.

"Sometimes, God needs us to be perfectly still before He can begin to do His work," I said. At that moment, one of my caregivers reached for the back of my wheelchair. I continued by explaining that what they were doing was coming in, at my request (yielding in the present), to turn off my chair, making it safe for them to do what day need to do. However, entrusting them to turn off power to my chair also meant I was completely and totally immobile. I like to parallel these moments to the times in our lives when nothing seems to be working and everything has appeared to stop progressing in the direction we would like. These "hard stop" moments are often those moments when some of life's events or compilation of decisions have brought us to a place of standstill. It is in these moments when I ask myself, as I am sure many others have also asked themselves, "Why can't I seem to get ahead?" or "Why does life seem to be passing me by?" Using my life as a visual aid, these answers started becoming clearer. The pursuit of yielding caused me to ask myself, "Could these be moments when God (the ultimate caregiver) has come in and turned off the power so He can start positioning us for our destiny?" It is this question that caused me to reflect back to the times of my life when "hard stop" moments have occurred.

Be still, and know that I am God: I will be exalted among the nations, I will be exalted in the earth. – Psalms 46:10 KJV

CHAPTER SEVEN
Hard Stops

In early 2013, I found myself at a mental and spiritual place I had never been before. For the first time in my life, I had suddenly reached the point where everything seemed to be in slow motion to the point it felt like life was standing still. There had been other times in my life where things were not perfect, or they were even challenging. This time, things felt different. It was as though everything I tried could not bring fulfillment. I was not enjoying my job, and it was a good one. I did not like going out with friends, and I like to think I am a social person. Even church seemed to be unfulfilling. The only way I can describe it is everything seemed to just stop. It felt as though life was going nowhere.

Little did I know my life had slowly coasted to a complete stop. I was working every day, and life was still happening. I just did not feel like life had any sense of direction. I would like to say this feeling was fleeting, but that would be a lie. In fact, this devoid feeling lasted for quite a few months. It was during this period in my life that I had one of the most powerful encounters with life and death I had ever had. It is the encounter I discussed earlier in this book about going into a coma. It is true; my physical body had quite literally found itself in the condition that my spiritual and emotional man had been carrying for months prior. It was this season of "hard stop" in my life that brought me to a point of stillness that would lead to the most powerful transition of my life.

"When God comes in and renders us immobile, we often find ourselves asking what we did to deserve the punishment," I stated as I continued sharing the parallels of what it looks like to yield when God is positioning us for transition into a new season. Although nearly two and a half years had passed between the time I was in a coma and the time I was in front of the audience for the first time sharing the message, the vulnerability and emotion I felt while describing this season while being immobile was indescribable. It literally took me two years to truly appreciate how valuable these seasons can be.

For the first time, I understood these times from a posture of love rather than one of a punitive nature. I no longer viewed the stillness or lack of progress as negative because I understood how to see God as a caregiver who renders us immobile so He can come in and change things or move us. "Please hear me tonight. These moments are not punitive; it is His way of loving us," I said with tears in my eyes. I could tell there were many people listening with questions arising in their minds. I, too, had the same questions. If it's not punitive, then why does it feel so negative? I used to think. Even now, as I write this book some three years later, I sometimes struggle to remember how much love these seasons contain.

Though my time was limited that evening, I did my best to explain what I have since taken time to develop and transcribe into this book and at subsequent speaking engagements. These times of "hard stops" are often perceived as negative because of fear. In many cases, the fear is the lack of belief that God truly has things under control. Other times, it is the fear of failing to achieve some unseen calling in an unknown timeframe. At other times, it is the fear of the unknown which can cause us to take risks or fail to take risks for fear of what lies ahead. These fears filter the way we look at times in our lives when things are still and peaceful. It is almost as though we look for a reason to stay active or stay in control.

In a literal sense, as a quadriplegic, if I chose to stay in control of my wheelchair and in continual motion, it would be almost impossible for me to get out of my chair. Not getting out of my chair would make it difficult to sleep, stretch out my body for rest, and ultimately, it could cause problems with skin breakdowns, resulting in immense pain. In much the same way, when we insist on staying busy or staying in control, it can result in mental, spiritual, and even physical unrest. I have even seen in my life where continual efforts to remain in control caused me to be emotionally inflexible and unable to stretch out my creativity or produce good work. In other instances, I have personally experienced emotional pain from the hurt I have caused by not being still enough to hear someone's heart or heed wisdom. If I can see the parallel between my physical body and my mental, emotional, and spiritual being needing times of rest, then why are they viewed so negatively? The answer is relatively simple: it is how I perceive the reason for the standstill.

I am sure there are many like me out of those who were there that first night I delivered the message on being yielded who had experienced seasons of exhaustion accompanied by the feeling of life coming to a complete standstill.

Well, what if it had all changed by choosing to yield? "Yield to what?" is a question one might ask. I know I did. What if the answer is this simple? What if it's a matter of yielding to the idea or belief that our Creator loves us enough to give us seasons of rest? What if these seasons can be perceived by our minds to be times of rejuvenation in preparation for a destiny we have not yet realized? Well, I believe they are just that. Just as my caregivers reach around to the back of my chair to shut off the power, rendering it safe to begin transitioning me from the chair to a place of rest, moments of "hard stop" can be the same. They can be moments where we choose to trust that there is a Creator who loves us enough to ensure our safety and positions us for the purposes He has created us to fulfill.

In Psalms 91, King David describes these moments by stating, "He that dwelleth in the secret place of the Most High shall abide under the shadow of the Almighty…" It is in these moments when King David acknowledges the revelation of God being a fortress, a refuge, and a very present help in the time of trouble. "Abiding under the shadow" suggests a place of rest. It is in this place where we often discover the true safety and might of God. This is a place one can only access with the revelation of love. It is the caring love of God that we must yield to for us to completely gain the benefit and peace that comes during these times.

Over the past few years, as I demonstrated this segment of the yielding process, I continued to gain a deeper understanding of how this concept of acknowledging the love of God is only the first step in one of the first areas we get to daily choose to yield to God. As I explained in my presentations, when a caregiver turns the main power off at the back of my chair, they are not only rendering me unable to maneuver from place to place, but they are also turning off my ability to adjust the recline, tilt, and lateral movement of the seat to my chair. This can represent how these times of immobility can also represent the sacrifice of comfort. Being unable to move directionally is one thing, but being unable to adjust one's body for comfortability is something completely different. Trusting God with the overall direction of our lives is something many people, including myself, feel like we do. We say our daily prayers and ask God to bless our food, to guide us, to give us wisdom, and sometimes even to "take the wheel." All these prayers can be deceiving to our minds and lead us to believe we are giving God control of the overall direction of our lives. What about our actions? Do we ever really yield our actions completely to His?

When I am in my power chair, there are two types of control. I have a mechanism (joystick) that enables me to control the direction the chair goes. I also have a switch that helps me control the positioning of my body within the chair. It gives me a sense of being able to adjust for comfort. However, when my caregivers turn off the power to the chair, then I am yielding both direction and comfort to them. "Yielding control to a God that cares for us looks much the same," I said as the caregivers continued the process of helping me get out of my chair. In the physical, it takes relationship building and trust to get to a place of choosing to allow someone to render you completely powerless, immobile, and out of control. In fact, to the human mind, this concept may seem unwise or even foolish. When we choose to yield to our supreme caregiver by establishing a relationship through prayer and devotional time with Him, giving control of our destiny and our present comfort is the wisest thing we can do. "Cast all your cares on Him... Be anxious for nothing, but in all things with prayer and supplication...

Take no thought for tomorrow for tomorrow will take care of itself…' are all familiar passages of Scripture we quote," I explained. Do we ever truly completely trust God to care for us in these areas?

As the sermon progressed, I could see the eyes of people in the crowd as they stared intently at the process my body was demonstrating. I could see the results of how their minds were processing the idea of yielding control and comfort. That evening, I explained how the parallel God had showed me to my own life had begun to cause me to reevaluate how much I had truly yielded control of my direction and my comfort to God. "Perhaps you are like me. Perhaps you have treated God as a consultant in your life rather than the CEO?" I asked myself these questions.

Now, I ask audiences around the world, and even the reader of this book, to ponder the same question. The truth is that we yield control of our direction and comfort to something. Some yield control of the comfort to an addiction to food, drugs, sex, or alcohol. It is not long before yielding our comfort to these things greatly affects our destiny. We like to tell ourselves how we are making conscious choices to ensure our success, but we often walk in the deception that we are the ones in control. The apostle Paul stated in the book of Romans that we are servants to whom we yield ourselves to obey. He also clearly delineates the two realms to which we can yield. We can yield to the realm of the flesh, or we can yield to the Spirit. It is either one or the other. There is no in-between. How is it we are so easily deceived into believing that there is "me?" It is God who gives us life. It is God who knows the beginning from the end. It is God who chose our time of birth. Why do I, and so many others, struggle to believe and trust a God with this much wisdom to care for us? I have spent my whole life hearing about God, serving in the church, reading the Bible, but now, the revelation and illumination of the need to yield to God in every area of my life has awakened a desire to pursue the peace and true power that comes when we yield to His Spirit. When we choose to say, "God, I know you love me and I trust You with my life."

The more I understand how the choice to allow my caregivers to assist me is what enables me to experience the most out of life, the more I understand the importance of allowing God to do the same. In the same way I need assistance in more than one area, we need assistance from our Creator in more than just our daily comfort and life's destiny. Yielding control of our direction and comfort is only the beginning of the process. We can sit or stand still in our uncomfortable state of being and never completely experience God's destiny for our lives because we choose not to yield in all areas. The parallels of me getting out of my chair continue to reveal many areas where the choice to yield to God's plan and purpose can bring fullfillment and peace. The next step in the process involves the removal of things that have become part of what I rely on to provide support and security to my head and limbs. In much the same way, God wants to remove things in our lives so we will rely on Him for support and security. He will often begin with the things we mentally rely on to bring us peace.

Let the words of my mouth, and the meditation of my heart, be acceptable in thy sight, O LORD, my strength, and my redeemer.

– Psalms 19:14 KJV

CHAPTER EIGHT
A Vocal Alignment

The audience's eyes were fixated on me. It was as though laser beams were piercing through the air and landing right on my chest as I continued speaking that night. "I suddenly realized it is not enough to just yield my life as a whole," I continued. "There are different aspects and areas of my life that needed to conform to the yielding process. For example, I use a headset microphone to amplify my voice when I'm doing a public presentation," I iterated. This microphone gives me comfort and an ability to maintain my voice. It also enables me to ensure I can be heard above any ambient noises. In much the same way, we become accustomed to having a voice in certain aspects of our life. When we are on our job, talking with our family, or simply speaking with a friend, we are accustomed to having a certain privilege or right to speak. However, rarely had I ever considered yielding my voice or the place that my voice had to God.

Sure, I have heard people speak from platforms and podiums about the power of the tongue. I have preached and heard preached messages about the importance of speaking life over death, but seldom had I ever stopped to consider the value of every word. The importance of understanding the value of aligning, not only our words, but the place or authority our voice carries, was now more real to me than ever.

Using my own microphone as an example, I demonstrated how if I am going to align myself with God (represented by my caregivers in the demonstration), I would have to choose to trust Him to remove the device that gave me power to be heard. I would have to trust Him to provide the voice and the power to be heard in the time that He chose. As my caregivers began to remove my microphone, it became obvious to the audience that without my headset microphone and the PA system it was attached to, it would be difficult for the message to be heard by everyone in the room. It is at this point in the message when a second caregiver steps in to hold a microphone to my mouth. I am now able to be heard. However, the microphone, its position, and the use of it is completely under the control of my caregiver who represents God in the example. If the microphone is moved away, the sound becomes diminished. If the microphone is moved closer, the sound becomes louder.

We often talk about giving our words and voice to God. We even sing songs about Him being the breath in our lungs, but do we really trust Him to be the power and the means by which we speak? This is the question I began to ask myself as the revelation of yielding became more real to me.

The caregiver holding the microphone moved it away. "Now you cannot hear me as well, but you can see that I am still speaking," I say to the audience. Just then, the caregiver brings the microphone back to where I can be heard. This is an amazing example of how we can be deceived into thinking because we are speaking and a few people can hear that we are reaching our maximum potential. In reality, we have been speaking in our own strength. There is strength and freedom that comes from knowing how to yield our voice to God.

Yielding our voice starts by acknowledging how He desires to give us a voice. Knowing His character and His Word that helps us to speak the way He would is vital. On the other hand, understanding His character and aligning ourselves to spend time with Him will allow us to understand the "when" to speak. We can begin to distinguish between speaking our will versus His, and we can learn the boldness that comes from silence when nothing is to be said. These moments are opportunities for our actions to be our voice. Much like the moments when the caregivers remove a microphone, moments of not being heard are opportunities for the message to be delivered by the actions of our lives. A vocal alignment with God requires an understanding that His breath gives us the ability to speak. His Word gives us the vocabulary, but our intimate relationship with Him gives us the ability to know when to speak.

The simplicity of yielding our voice to Him is demonstrated by giving Him place in every conversation. It is revealed by intentionally asking Him what He wants to say. It is fulfilled by allowing Him to speak through us in a manner that brings Him honor and glory. For far too long, the focus has been on the power of life and death being in the tongue. While this is scripturally sound and spiritually accurate, it is quite incomplete. When one seeks to understand the power of life and death, they must also seek to understand the relationship value with the One who gives life and death. In short, knowing the power is not as fulfilling as being plugged in to the power source. If we can truly plug into the source and yield our speech, it will not be long before we begin to look at our works and deeds. Yielding our voice opens the door for us to further understand how to yield what we do to the power source.

And whatsoever ye do in word or deed, do all in the name of the Lord Jesus, giving thanks to God and the Father by him.

– Colossians 3:17 KJV

CHAPTER NINE
Aligning Our Works

As a child, I can remember times when I would meet a total stranger. At least they were a total stranger to me. However, they would be friends of either one of my parents. Very often, I would hear these individuals say something like, "Oh! You act just like your mom!" Sometimes I would hear my mother say something like, "You are acting just like your father!" I'm sure many people have had these types of experiences. It is in these experiences that I found a nugget of truth. I realized that when these statements were being made, the individual making them was often attributing my actions (works) to the individual they felt I had most learned to emulate.

Truth be told, we emulate through our works that which we spend time with. What we spend time with is almost always what we trust or value. This emulation is yet another example of yielding. The Bible instructs us whatsoever we do, do all in the name of Jesus. Pursuing understanding, I began to research the word "name." I discovered that the word "name" did not necessarily signify the actual written word of a name. For example, to do something in the name of Jennifer does not signify that one is supposed to change the name, by which they are known, to Jennifer. Rather, doing something in the name of another individual means to walk in the character, authority, or delegated power of that individual.

In the early days of kings and kingdoms, if someone came bearing the name of a king, it usually signified that they were walking as a representative or an ambassador of that king. To state or to act in a manner contrary to the king's character would often result in the individual's demise. In much the same way, an individual who had been raised or trained in the house of a king or ruler was also expected to conduct themselves in a manner that would reflect or constitute an understanding of whose kingdom they belonged to. For this to happen, an individual would often have to choose to abide by this character. They would swear an oath that their actions and deeds would be fitting of the king or kingdom they represented. Often times these individuals would be asked, "Will you yield?"

As I continued my message that evening, I shared the revelation of the importance for us to yield our works. We live as eternal beings, serving an eternal King and believe we will reign in His eternal kingdom with Him, but have we truly chosen to yield to His character? Have we acknowledged the demonstration of Him in our works or our deeds while we are yet living in our mortality? That night, as I posed these questions, I continued by sharing how these questions have convicted me. They have prompted me to remember that being a child of God means His DNA and His character should be reflected in my identity. Why is it that His character is not reflected in my identity through my works? It is due to failing to yield. Though I have DNA and the opportunity to be in the presence of the King, I am still given the opportunity to choose to yield my works and actions. What does that look like? Again, I go back to the example of my own frailty. My body is so weak that my actions require the help of others to accomplish them. If I want to move my arms or legs, I get to choose to trust caregivers to move them. I get to trust that they will know what I have need of and be mindful of what I can handle in the way of movement and pain.

Demonstrating what it looks like to yield our works, I continued speaking that night about what it is like to have someone move your arms and legs. Though I was in my power chair, my arms and legs were in comfortable positions. If I wanted to move beyond the position I was in, I would get to choose to allow my caregivers to come in and begin to move or position my arms and legs. My arms and legs represent the works and deeds of our lives. My caregivers represent the enabling power of God. It is His grace that gives us the ability to do anything. It is our faith and trust in Him that will determine the level to which He is involved in our works.

Many times, we will sit in a place of comfort to

the point that our bodies become stiff and sore. Our works become rigid. Our character becomes wrought with traditionalism or religious repetition. It is not long before we often feel stuck, going through actions and never really moving anywhere. It is in these times where we have the opportunity to choose to yield to the realization that we are kings and priests serving under the highest King with His DNA running through our veins. He will begin to come in, much like my caregivers do, and reposition our works and deeds to prepare us for where He is taking us. It is His desire for us to demonstrate His power, His mannerisms, and His glory. As He begins to sculpt and mold our works, we begin to prepare to move from where we are by allowing Him access to the vital parts of our emotions. It is at this point where we begin to understand that our works, when aligned and yielded to God will take us places we could never imagine or think. This means we get to choose to yield our inward parts or our vitals to Him.

Behold, thou desirest truth in the inward parts: and in the hidden part thou shalt make me to know wisdom.

– *Psalms 51:6 KJV*

CHAPTER TEN

Exposing Your Vitals

The experiences of life bring with them some ups and downs, some pains and relief, and often some wounds and scars. These experiences often result in an unintentional attempt to protect ourselves from future negative feelings or emotions. This protection can take on many forms and fashions. For some, it may look like isolation. Others may attempt to protect themselves by shutting off certain emotions. In some cases, these protections can result in years of attempts to numb or cover wounds by addictive behaviors. No matter the approach toward protection, all of these protective acts tend to have one thing in common. They serve as perceived support, and even barriers, to the vital places of our emotions.

I would like to believe, for me, that there has never been a situation where I needed to rely on such protection, but this simply would not be true. As I mentioned earlier in this book, I had spent years burying myself alive beneath mounds of self-doubt and self-loathing. Although I had allowed God to help me dig out of this self-made grave, I rarely ever let the complete protective barrier around the inward parts of my emotions and heart to become completely exposed. Now, more than ever, I was beginning to understand how easy it is to be free on the outside while allowing the innermost parts of me to remain bound. I began to understand how I had chosen to allow my heart and emotions to be protected by prejudices, misguided opinions, resentment, anger, sarcasm, jokes, and other habits. It was now time for me to choose to yield the vulnerable parts of my heart to the will and purpose of God. The process of how I get out of my wheelchair is a great example of what it takes to allow God to remove the things that we perceive to bring comfort. If I truly want to be moved out of my chair, I need to allow my caregivers to remove the chest strap which holds my upper body upright. This strap spans across my chest, covering my lungs, heart, and several ribs. In the physical, I am allowing my caregivers to remove the only thing that both holds me safely in the chair and covers/protects my most vital organs.

Symbolically, my caregivers are removing the things that bring me a sense of security and protection. In much the same way, when we yield to God and ask Him to remove everything that keeps us from being all He wants us to be, we are often faced with a decision of whether or not we are willing to allow our spiritual and emotional vitals to be exposed. For some, this could look like letting go of past hurts. It may also look like aligning a way of thinking about the past to the Word of God. It may even look like letting go of external habits or means of comfort, such as smoking, drinking, gambling, over-eating, sexual addictions, and any other vice we depend on for support or protection from unpleasant experiences or emotions. This "letting go" process often begins with an acknowledgment that we are ready to let go of the things we depend on or are addicted to and are ready to yield to the love and heart of God.

Exposing my vitals is the final step in allowing my caregivers to be completely in control of my position, protection, and placement. As my body falls limp into the arms of my caregivers, I am yielding completely to their strength and protection. This process can be uncomfortable and unsettling if there is any doubt or mistrust between my caregivers and me. It is at this point when the control of what makes me comfortable is no longer within my own abilities. This is what it can feel like when we ask God to remove all of our supports and protections in order to completely yield to His control.

It is a process that can feel quite uncomfortable to our emotions and spirit. While uncomfortable, we cry out to our supreme caregiver to take us into His arms. It is an act of leaving what we are comfortable with to embrace the unknown.

Now the LORD had said unto Abram, Get thee out of thy country, and from thy kindred, and from thy father's house, unto a land that I will shew thee: And I will make of thee a great nation, and I will bless thee, and make thy name great; and thou shalt be a blessing:

– Genesis 12:1-2 KJV

CHAPTER ELEVEN
Leaving the Comfort Zone to Find Comfort

Returning to the example of my body and life as a visual aid, I want to take this time to explain, explore, and expound on what it is like to put complete and total control in the hands of something or someone more powerful than oneself. Almost everyone over the age of six months qualifies as physically stronger and more physically able than I am. This means my life often requires the physical strength and ability of others in order to accomplish life's basic functions. For example, if I need to go to the restroom or get into bed, it is someone else's strength and ability that makes this happen. They must pick me up, remove or add clothing, clean me and position me. The challenge in these endeavors is whether or not the person helping me to accomplish these things will do them in a way that is not painful, in a way that would bring me comfort, and in a way I would choose if I was doing it myself. As one can imagine, finding this type of person is difficult. Not only is it difficult to find a person who can be "others minded," it also requires me to be open to trusting them with the most intimate parts of me.

Sometimes, it is easy to see someone interact with others and determine if they have a level of compassion. It is not always easy to determine if someone has the ability to open up and serve someone at their point of comfort and need. It is a balancing act. Someone who is truly compassionate may also have a strong desire to help someone avoid possible self-inflicted or unforeseen pitfalls. With every well-meaning intent, the individual providing compassion and care can often slip into a control position. This type of control can often result in not allowing the individual to experience the growth that comes from making mistakes. It is often in these types of moments that relationships find themselves in moments that I like to call "yielding opportunities." Both the caregiver and the one receiving care are challenged to yield to something. For many years, I personally felt that true care was when a caregiver yielded only to what I needed or wanted.

It is only now that I realize it is not about yielding to one another's will or way. It is about yielding to purpose. The purpose may be short-term or long-term in nature, but when both parties are clear and communication has been conveyed, the choice to yield becomes about accomplishing a task together rather than competing for power or a battle of wills. How did I ever arrive at this new depth of understanding? It all traces back to that moment several years ago when I was asked the question, "Will you yield?" I wasn't only being asked if I would align my eternal soul to an eternal destination. I wasn't only being asked to yield my daily activities, my emotions, or my thoughts. I was being asked if I was willing to be in a relationship where I could be moved from what was comfortable and in my control to an uncomfortable place of journeying with the One who cares, knows all, and sees the ultimate purpose ahead.

There is an old song that I grew up singing entitled, "Because He Lives, I Can Face Tomorrow." The lyrics of this song say that He holds the future. It is amazing how much we believe He created all things. We believe He holds the future, but when it comes to holding us and carrying us to our divine purpose, we often feel as though it should be done in a way that brings us comfort or the way we would do it. The truth of the matter is, this type of mindset often causes us to remain stagnant and imprisoned by our own comfort.

When my caregivers have removed the chest strap from my body, and I find myself being supported by only their arms, the realization of inevitable change becomes real. The choice to remain in my chair would become more uncomfortable than simply choosing to allow the caregivers to continue moving me from where I am to where we are purposed to go. This is one of the most exciting yet unsettling experiences. It is in this moment when I realize that the control of my comfort is completely in the strength and ability of someone else. It is also the moment when I realize that going back would require depending on fixed and inanimate objects for my comfort.

In much the same way, when life brings us to a point where habits, hurts, or addictions are being stripped away, we must choose to move from the past into the present. We often must also realize how moving to our purpose will require allowing something more powerful and more able to carry us from our place of stagnant comfort into a place of true peace. What makes this concept even more unsettling is the amount of relationship building and understanding needed to truly overcome the fear of leaving what seems safe to embrace the unknown.

As the caregiver begins to lift me out of my chair, my sense of safety comes from the relationship built prior. In my life, there are many people who offer to help and have great hearts, yet I am an individual who wants to know that a person is not only caring, but able. It often takes a few weeks, if ever, for me to work up the trust or comfort level to allow someone to carry me. Some might call it fear; others might call it wisdom. Whatever it is called, it is definitely a time of building trust and faith. Once I have been able to feel the strength and heart of an individual, I am more open to trusting them with the most intimate part of my care. "Total control" is the most intimate type of care one can receive or provide. Though I use my physical body and daily life as an image for this concept, it is no comparison to the true love affair that we should develop with our Creator. We need a posture of love that says, "I give You all of me." We can look at the transition from our comfort to His purpose as uncomfortable, or we can realize that this process is one of the deepest levels of intimacy we can ever experience.

He that dwelleth in the secret place of the most High shall abide under the shadow of the Almighty. I will say of the LORD, He is my refuge and my fortress: my God; in him will I trust. – Psalms 91:1-2 KJV

CHAPTER TWELVE

The Intimacy Involved in Trusting the Process

With one arm behind my neck and the other under my legs, the caregiver lifted me from my chair with gentle ease. The audience looked ever intently as a microphone is held over the shoulder of my caregiver, and I continued to speak. "You see when I am carried or lifted from my chair, my eyes can only see the face of my caregiver, and my heart can feel their heartbeat," I continued. You could hear a pin drop in the room. More than 300 people stared and listened intently to every word as I continued to describe what it is like to be completely at the mercy of someone else's care. This is a type of care that brings with it the understanding of how much the one holding me loves me and the revelation that the depth of my ability to love them is reflected in how much I am able to rest in their arms.

Many of us, as believers, will state how much we trust and depend on God, yet in times of transition where His arms are carrying us, we tend to panic and fear. We cannot see what lies ahead because our face is upon His shoulder and our eyes are gazing at His countenance. It is in these moments when we realize He is looking forward and holding our future. We often struggle with not knowing and having the faith to trust what we cannot see. Just like the example of me being carried by a caregiver, it is in these moments of transition where we begin to truly understand whether or not we are yielded to a posture of love for Him. We can see and grasp His love for us. We can feel His strength. We can see His face. We can even gain comfort by knowing that our hearts are aligned with His. Do we love Him enough to trust that, though we cannot see the future, He sees and knows all?

Being carried by someone else reveals one other spiritual truth about yielding from a posture of love. It is the intimacy that is created through the communication between the one being carried and the one carrying. In relation to God, it is our opportunity to let our requests be made known and to rest in the idea that if we can feel His heart, He feels ours. This means our anxiety is felt before we can even speak. Because of His love for us, He begins to act on our behalf. I wonder if this is why the scripture tells us to "be anxious for nothing." I also wonder if the hidden truth to this passage isn't further revealed in the portion that directs us to let our requests be made known through prayer and supplication.

You see, when someone is carrying me, I simply need to convey to them where I'd like to go. My relationship with them reveals how I would like to be handled or positioned. Their strength, ability, and compassion to care is what makes the bond of intimacy and trust secure. Knowing that they hear and love me is what makes the ability to yield to the idea of being completely in their control so possible and pleasant.

Delighting in the intimacy of our Creator is what makes the journey of life worth the effort. Trusting Him to be our ultimate caregiver and knowing the depth of His love is what enables us to activate purpose in our lives by resting in the identity of His desire to carry us to our destiny. Yielding completely to Him is the key to unlocking the ability for us to arrive at the destination of our ignited destiny.

Now the Lord is that Spirit: and where the Spirit of the Lord is, there is liberty. – *2 Corinthians 3:17 KJV*

CHAPTER THIRTEEN
Destination of Destiny

Experiencing the feeling of rendering my total and complete movements to someone else is a feeling to which I have become accustomed. It is, for me, an everyday part of life. This part of life is greatly affected when the relationship between my caregivers and me are either good or bad. The ways it is affected is usually determined by how well communication, trust, and understanding have been developing between us during our times of growth together. When there is ever a change in caregivers, the level of effectiveness in being completely vulnerable and open to trust can be quite the challenge. This is because of the unknowns within the relationship in the beginning stages. My caregivers and I go through a season of developing trust and communication. It is the development of this symbiotic relationship of intimacy that impacts, not only the journey, but also the destination. Developing trust through intimacy and love has proven to be a fundamental necessity in my life. How this trust affects the process and, ultimately, the destination or outcome is what so many of us often struggle with throughout the journey called "life".

As I continued with the demonstration of using my

physical limitations and life experiences to show the revelation of yielding, the caregiver held me like one would hold a baby. The audience continued to watch as I explained the parallels of being held by God. It is in this time of holding where we experience another degree of intimacy with Him. As I mentioned previously, we can see His face and feel His heartbeat. That alone is intimacy. There is still another aspect of intimacy revealed. It is the realization of the magnitude of His love and strength. It is also the intimacy of choosing to trust Him to take us where we are purposed to go in life's journey.

As I continued speaking to the audience, my caregiver who was holding me began to move from a position next to my wheelchair and took me to a resting place on a massage table that had been prepared for me to lay. While carrying me to the resting place, I continued to explain how our part in this loving relationship of trust and yielding is to make our request known. It is also to understand that as we delight in His love for us, He knows what we need before we ask.

"Lord, you see where I've been."
"You know where You want me to go."
"You have created me for a purpose."
"I trust you with my life and the ultimate purpose of it."

These are examples of prayers we might give when being held by Him and carried by Him during certain periods of our lives. The good thing about relying on Him to be our ultimate caregiver is that He will never leave us. There is no changing of caregivers. This means that as we build a relationship with Him, the only change will come if we choose to yield our thoughts or our lives to some other form of care besides Him. He will carry us to places we never knew we could experience. The psalmist, David, said, "He makes me to lie down in green pastures and leads me besides still waters…" His care for us will take us to places of peace. Just as my caregiver takes me to a table where I can lay and rest, so also will God take us to places of peace and rest.

As my caregiver placed me on the table, I continued to speak about how I have not only been brought to a place of rest, but I was also being positioned in a place of comfort. My caregiver knew my needs so well that I could continue speaking while he adjusted my arms and legs into positions of comfort and rest. The Heavenly Father knows us so well that He can do the same. As I reached the conclusion of my example, the audience witnessed how my caregiver stood over me as I spoke. In this moment, I let them know how our God will also stand over us. "King David describes it in the 91st chapter of Psalms when he said, 'He that dwells in the secret place of the Most High shall abide under the shadow of the Almighty,'" I explained to the audience. In that moment, I also demonstrated the power of resting in the destination He has taken us to.

Holding back the tears, I managed to start singing a

song of worship. As I began to sing, I could see the audience begin to emotionally respond. In the middle of singing, I shared with them how being in the place of rest with Him is the ultimate place to be. It is a destination where our worship of Him becomes our most powerful warfare, and we begin to truly understand and know Him as a strong tower and a fortress. Because He has taken us to this place, we can say He is our God and in Him we will trust. Seeing the visual of me laying on the table representing humankind and seeing my caregiver standing over me with love, the audience began to weep.

For whosoever will save his life shall lose it: and whosoever will lose his life for my sake shall find it. – *Matthew 16:25 KJV*

CHAPTER FOURTEEN
The Posture of Living in Love

"It's your breath in my lungs, so I pour out my praise, pour out my praise…" I began to sing. The more I sang, the more I felt the intensity rising within myself. In all honesty, for a brief moment, it was as though the audience was no longer there. I had transcended into a place of complete intimacy with God. As I concluded the "Yielded" message that night for the first time, it was as though the past few years had culminated into the deepest revelation of my life. Yielding was not a one-time act. It was a posture. It was a choice. It was a way of living. It was all of these things. It was a way of love.

Mustering my composure, I opened my eyes while singing and began to speak to the audience as the music continued to play. At this point, it was no longer me speaking. The words that were coming out of my mouth seemed to be coming from a place beyond my human comprehension. The past few years of wrestling with the question asked of me while in a coma was now becoming so clear. It was a question to me that was not only for me, but for the world. That night, I asked the audience that same question, and I now ask you, the reader. Will you yield?

That night the audience responded in a way I did not expect. "We have a supreme caregiver who loves us so much," I said through tear-filled eyes. "He wants to remove everything that holds us back from His divine purpose. He wants to take us to a place of rest and safety while holding us safely in His arms," I continued with an invitation by asking if there was anyone in the room who was ready to "yield". This was an invitation to not only yield in terms of salvation, but also in terms of loving Him as our caregiver. It was also an invitation to live in a posture of love every day, which requires the daily choice to trust Him with every part of our lives.

Before I could finish the question, people all over the auditorium were weeping and acknowledging that they were ready. I prompted them, as I do the reader of this book, to find a physical position of yielding. It could be laying on the floor, bowing a knee, bowing a head, or any other form of acknowledging His love. That night, nearly everyone in the room was laying on the floor yielding their lives to the One who is love.

Little did I know how much one question could change the way I look at my relationship with God. Living my whole life as a "Christian," I had never fully understood the power of choosing a relationship with Him from love. I didn't realize how much fear of loss, of getting hurt, of not being in control, of not being accepted, and even the fear of not going to heaven was more of my motivation to serve Him. One question changed it all. One question led me down the path that ultimately inspired me to write this book. That one question ignited a deeper relationship with my Creator. It gave me a deeper understanding of His love and how He chose to yield to the cross because of His love for us. I now choose to yield because of my love for Him. Daily, I am inspired to allow love to be the power behind my choice to align with His purpose. I choose love to be my reason for trusting that where I am is where He has taken me. He protects. He holds. He carries. He supplies. He directs. He loves. Knowing this, I leave you with the question I was asked in 2013. A question asked by my Creator was a question, that if answered with love and in love, will change your life and potentially the world.

Will you yield?

About the Author

As an inspirational and motivational speaker, Howard Bell has lived his life sharing the message that physical, mental, and emotional limitations do not have to determine identity or purpose. Instead, Howard has developed the lifestyle and belief that our identity and purpose, if well cultivated, can unlock an amazing destiny.

At the age of one, Howard was diagnosed with Infantile Spinal Muscular Atrophy. His prognosis was fatal. Doctors had told his parents he would probably not live beyond the age of five, at best, into his early teens. As people of faith, Howard's parents and family chose to treat him as "normal" and encourage him to believe he had a divine purpose, and his identity rested in what he believed, not in what others said about him.

Now, more than four decades later, Howard has taken his life's story around the world to help encourage and inspire others. His passion and drive for seeing others succeed is what continues to fan the flames of purpose in his life that is unlocking the destiny in others everywhere.

Despite his physical challenges, Howard has accomplished many professional and personal goals, such as receiving a bachelor's degree from ASU with Summa Cum Laude and he was recently presented with an Honorary Doctorate Degree of Theology from Arizona-USA Christian University. He has also been appointed by governors and mayors to serve on various community and political boards. Howard has been a spokesperson for the Easter Seals Society. He has been the Vice President and Chief Operating Officer for various corporations in the field of education. He is a published author and has been featured on TBN and the 700 Club along with several radio programs throughout the U.S. Howard was also the host of the *More Than A Conqueror* radio program for four years, spanning Arizona, New Mexico, Nevada, and parts of California.

Today, Howard travels and speaks in churches, businesses, institutions, schools, and at various community organizations throughout the world. His mission is to reach the globe with the message that there are no limits for those who believe.

"If I can do it, weighing 45 pounds and having no strength in my arms and legs, then you can, too."

CPSIA information can be obtained
at www.ICGtesting.com
Printed in the USA
BVHW061949221221
624600BV00013B/1515